Dear Parent:

Buckle up! You are about to join your child on a very exciting journey. The destination? Independent reading!

Road to Reading will help you and your child get there. The program offers books at five levels, or Miles, that accompany children from their first attempts at reading to successfully reading on their own. Each Mile is paved with engaging stories and delightful artwork.

Getting Started

For children who know the alphabet and are eager to begin reading
• easy words • fun rhythms • big type • picture clues

Reading With Help

For children who recognize some words and sound out others with help
• short sentences • pattern stories • simple plotlines

Reading On Your Own

For children who are ready to read easy stories by themselves
• longer sentences • more complex plotlines • easy dialogue

First Chapter Books

For children who want to take the plunge into chapter books
• bite-size chapters • short paragraphs • full-color art

Chapter Books

For children who are comfortable reading independently
• longer chapters • occasional black-and-white illustrations

There's no need to hurry through the Miles. Road to Reading is designed without age or grade levels. Children can progress at their own speed, developing confidence and pride in their reading ability no matter what their age or grade.

So sit back and enjoy the ride—every Mile of the way!

With love
to my grandchildren
in order of appearance—
Cheyenne, Jazmyn, and Gregory
S.K.W.

To Carter
L.C.

Library of Congress Cataloging-in-Publication Data
Welch, Sheila Kelly.
Little Prince Know-It-All / by Sheila Kelly Welch ; illustrated by Lynne Cravath.
    p. cm. — (Road to reading. Mile 3)
Summary: Prince Caleb triumphs over his spoiled brother Omar when his parrot
becomes the cleverest pet in the kingdom.
ISBN 0-307-26301-0 (pbk.)
[1. Princes—Fiction. 2. Brothers—Fiction. 3. Parrots—Fiction.
4. Pets—Fiction.] I. Cravath, Lynne, ill. II. Title.
III. Series.
PZ7.W44894Li 1998
[E]—dc21   98-5795
                                                            CIP
                                                            AC

A GOLDEN BOOK • New York
Golden Books Publishing Company, Inc. New York, New York 10106

ISBN: 0-307-26301-0
                                            A MCMXCVIII

Little Prince Know-It-All

by Sheila Kelly Welch
illustrated by Lynne Cravath

Once there were two princes

who lived so long ago

your great-great-greatest-grandparents

would not have known them.

Caleb was the older

of the two princes.

He was a kind and thoughtful boy.

His younger brother, Omar,

was just the opposite.

Omar was terribly spoiled.

But no one in the palace

seemed to notice.

Except Caleb, of course.

And Caleb kept his mouth shut.

When it was time to eat breakfast,

Omar always said,

"Give me the biggest slice

of pomegranate bread."

And he got it.

When it was time to ride

the royal horses,

Omar always said,

"I want the fastest horse!"

And he got to ride Pegasus.

When it was time for dinner,

Omar always said,

"Let's have roast eggplant!"

And the cook would roast eggplant

and serve it on

the royal purple plates,

because Omar liked those plates

better than the gold ones.

Poor Caleb hated eggplant

on *any* color plate.

He wished just once

he could get the best of Omar.

One day Omar said to Caleb,

"There are hundreds of animals

in our kingdom.

But not one belongs to us."

"Us?" asked Caleb.

"Yes, us," said Omar.

"We are the royal princes.

Yet we have no pet of our own.

Our mother owns Powder Puff,

the royal cat.

Our father owns Pegasus,

the fastest horse in the kingdom."

Omar frowned.

"Even the boys of the village

have pets to call their own,"

he said.

Caleb did not think

the scraggly donkeys that carried

firewood for the village boys

could be called *pets*.

But he knew better than to argue

with Little Prince Know-It-All.

17

"I have an idea," said Omar.

"Let's get a pet lion!"

Caleb shook his head.

He knew what would happen.

When it came time to walk the lion,

he would be the one

dragged through the village.

And when the lion ate

some poor village boy,

he would take the blame.

"I know," said Omar.

"Let's get a giraffe!"

Caleb shook his head again.

When it came time to brush

the giraffe's teeth,

he would be the one

teetering on the ladder.

Caleb was even more

afraid of heights

than of his little brother.

"Well, how about an elephant?"

said Omar.

"We could ride him

all over the kingdom."

For just a moment,

Caleb liked that idea.

Then he thought about

the elephant's stall.

Not even Omar

could make the royal stablemen

clean an elephant's stall.

When it came time to do it,

Caleb was sure

he would be the one shoveling.

Caleb shook his head once more.

"How about if we each get

our own pet?" he said.

Omar smiled.

"That's a great idea, big brother.

My pet will be the cleverest

in the kingdom.

It will be much more clever

than your pet!"

Caleb smiled, too.

"Oh, no, it won't.

My pet will *talk*!"

"Pets can't talk!"

cried Know-It-All Omar.

But he looked just a tiny bit worried.

The very next morning,

a plump, squirmy puppy arrived

in Prince Omar's royal bedroom.

That same morning,

a colorful, long-tailed parrot arrived

in Prince Caleb's royal bedroom.

Right away, Caleb began trying

to teach his parrot to talk.

"Hello! Hello!" he said.

The parrot ruffled her feathers.

"How are you today?" said Caleb.

The parrot pecked his fingers.

"Polly want a cracker?" he said.

The parrot spat birdseed in his face.

Day after day, Caleb tried.

But the parrot sat in her cage

with her beak clamped shut.

While this was going on,
Omar's puppy grew
more and more clever.

"Sit!" said Omar.

The puppy sat.

"Fetch!" said Omar,

tossing a red ball.

The puppy chased after it.

"Drop it!" said Omar.

The puppy opened his mouth
and dropped the ball
right at Omar's feet.

"Stay!" said Omar.

The puppy stayed and stayed.

"I have the cleverest pet

in the kingdom!"

Omar bragged.

Caleb kept his mouth shut.

So—of course—did his parrot.

One fine day,

the king and queen announced

that the whole royal family

was going to visit

the kingdom next door.

Omar fed his puppy

and gave him a bowl of fresh water.

Caleb put clean parchment

on the bottom of his parrot's cage

and extra birdseed in her feeder.

"Hurry, big brother!"

called Omar.

"The royal carriage is about to leave.

I get the seat by the window!"

Caleb ran out the palace door.

Suddenly he stopped.

He had forgotten to lock
his parrot's cage!
"Wait for me!" he called
to the royal coachman.
He ran back into the palace.

Meanwhile, the parrot was busy.

She pushed open her cage door

and flew into the long palace hallway.

There, she began pecking

at the gold threads in the rug.

She didn't hear Omar's puppy

gallop into the hallway.

She didn't see him lick his lips.

But she *did* feel his teeth

close around her leg!

At that very moment,

Caleb came running around the corner.

He could not believe his eyes!

Before he could move,

or even say a word,

he heard a loud, raspy voice.

"DROP IT!"

squawked the voice.

The puppy opened his mouth,

just as he had been trained to do.

Out flew the parrot.

"SIT!" squawked the parrot.

The puppy sat.

"STAY!" squawked the parrot.

The puppy stayed and stayed.

Caleb laughed.

He knew his clever parrot was safe.

He waved good-bye

and ran out to the royal coach.

That afternoon,

when the royal family came home,

Omar was surprised.

His puppy was in the hallway,

fetching the red ball for the parrot!

"HELLO! HELLO!"

squawked the parrot.

"PRINCESS WANTS A CRACKER!"

Caleb grinned.

He ran to the royal pantry

and brought back all the crackers

he could carry.

From then on,

Caleb was happy.

Omar still got the biggest slice

of pomegranate bread.

He still rode Pegasus every day.

And he still had eggplant

whenever he wanted it.

But Caleb didn't care.

He knew that he had finally

gotten the best of his little brother.

He knew that his parrot

was the cleverest pet

in the kingdom.

But Caleb just smiled

and kept his mouth shut.